Land of Rocks and Lochs

A Guide to Assynt and Lochinver

First published in Great Britain by
Galatea (UK) Ltd
Kylesku, by Lairg, Sutherland, IV27 4HW

ISBN 1-898151-00-8

Printed by Highland Printers Ltd., Inverness

Land of Rocks and Lochs

A Guide to Assynt and Lochinver

Edited by Nick Kerr

Climbing Suilven

I nod and nod to my own shadow and thrust
A mountain down and down.
Between my feet a loch shines in the brown,
Its silver paper crinkled and edged with rust.
My lungs say No;
But down and down this treadmill hill must go.

Parishes dwindle. But my parish is
This stone, that tuft, this stone
And the cramped quarters of my flesh and bone.
I claw that tall horizon down to this;
And suddenly
My shadow jumps huge miles away from me.

Norman MacCaig

Failte gu Asainte
Welcome to Assynt

In welcoming you to Assynt, we, who live here, wish you, our visitor, a happy and memorable stay. We welcome you to magnificent coastal and mountain scenery, exciting wildlife and a crofting culture rich in Gaelic song and story.

Visitors are often unaware of how much there is to see, do and learn in Assynt. This Guide should enrich your stay, which may be too short to enjoy all we suggest. But we shall be happy to welcome you back another year. At home, in the winter, we hope you will enjoy this book as a reminder of happy days in Assynt.

As I write, the crofters of Assynt have made history. On 8th December, 1992, the Assynt Crofters' Trust succeeded in purchasing the North Lochinver Estate, thereby obtaining control over their own land.

The life in this beautiful land is active and lively, and we hope you take the time to savour it.

Madeline Macphail
Chairman, Assynt Tourism Group

Bienvenue à Assynt

Nous, habitants du pays d'Assynt, saurons vous y accueillir chaleureusement, et vous souhaitons un séjour agréable et inoubliable. Nous vous invitons à découvrir nos magnifiques paysages montagneux et côtiers et notre faune incomparable, et nous saurons vous faire apprécier notre culture riche en chant et foklore celtiques et centrée sur la pratique du "crofting"*.

Les visiteurs ignorent souvent la grande variété des choses à voir, à faire et à apprendre dans notre pays. Ce guide a été écrit pour enrichir votre séjour, qui sera peut-être trop court pour profiter de toutes nos suggestions. Mais nous serions très heureux de vous accueillir à nouveau une prochaine année. Nous espérons qu'à votre retour, durant l'hiver, ce livre vous fera revivre les jours hereux que vous aurez passés dans notre pays.

A l'heure où je rédige ce texte, les "crofters" d'Assynt vivent des jours historiques. Le 8 décembre 1992, le Assynt Crofters' Trust (Association des crofters de Assynt) a réussi à acheter le domain de North Lochinver. Ainsi, pour la première fois, les crofters auront la possibilité de gèrer eux mêmes leurs propres biens.

Dans ce beau pays, la vie est pétillante et gaie, et nous espérons que vous prendrez le temps de la savourer.

Madeline Macphail
Présidente
Groupement Touristique de Assynt

* crofting p12

Willkommen in Assynt

Die Einwohner von Assynt heißen Sie wiillkommen und wünschen Ihnen einen angenehmen und erlebnisreichen Aufenthalt. Sie finden bei uns eine herrliche Küsten - und Berglandschaft, eine artenreiche Fauna und eine blühende "Crofting"-Kulture* mit ihren gälischen Liedern und Erzählungen.

Den Besuchern bleibt oft verborgen, wiewiel es in Assynt eigentlich zu sehen, zu tun und zu entdecken gibt. Dieser Führer soll Ihnen helfen, Ihren Aufenthalt abwechslungsreicher zu gestalten. Wenn der Aufenthalt zu kurz ist, um alle unsere Vorschläge in die Tat umsetzen zu können, würden wir uns freuen, Sie wieder einmal bei uns begrüßen zu dürfen. An den langen Winterabenden zu Hause soll Sie dieses Buch an glückliche Tage in Assynt errinern.

Geraade in diesen Tagen haben die "Crofters" in Assynt Geschichte gemacht. Am 8 Dezember 1992 gelang es dem Crofterverband Assynts, die Ländereien von North Lochinver zu kaufen und dadurch die Kontrolle über ihr eigenes Land zu erhalten.

Das Leben in diesem schönen Landstrich ist abwechslungsreich und vielfältig, und wir hoffen, daß Sie sich die Zeit nehmen, es richtig zu genießen.

Madeline Macphail
Vorsitzende
Verkehrsverein Assynt

Bienvenido a Assynt

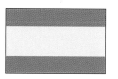

Al darte la bienvenida, te deseamos una feliz estancia entre nosotros. Te invitamos a recorrer nuestros bellas costas y montañas, a disfrutar de nuestra incomparable fauna y de una cultura basada en el crofting*, rica en canciones y leyendas gaélicas.

A menudo, quienes nos visitan desconocen la enorme variedad de cosas que se pueden ver, hacer y aprender en Assynt. Por eso, esta guía está pensada para que tu estancia entre nosotros sea más enriquecedora, aunque no dispongas del tiempo suficiente para disfrutar de todo lo que te proponemos. Siempre puedes volver en otra ocasión y, además, te queda este libro que esperamos sea un grato recuerdo de estos días.

En el momento de redactar estas líneas los crofters de Assynt viven jornadas históricas. El 8 de diciembre de 1992 la asociación de agricultores (Assynt crofters' Trust) ha logrado adquirir la finca de North Lochinver, consiguiendo así por primera vez el control de la tierra.

Este bello lugar está lleno de vida y esperamos que tengas el tiempo suficiente para saborearla.

> Madeline Macphail
> Presidenta
> Assynt Tourist Group

Benvenuti ad Assynt

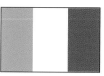

Nell'accoglierVi calorosamente nel nostro paese di Assynt, noi che ci abitiamo Vi auguriamo un soggiorno felice e indimenticabile. Vi invitiamo ad approfittare dei suoi magnifici paesaggi di montagna e di mare, della sua fauna caratteristica e della sua cultura basata sulle tradizioni del crofting* ricca di canti e storie celtici.

I turisti spesso ignorano quanto c'è da vedere, da fare e da imparare nel nostro paese. Cosi, questa guida è destinata ad arricchire il Vostro soggiorno che sarà forse troppo breve per approfittare di tutti i nostri suggerimenti. In quel caso, saremo felici di riospitarVi un altro anno. Al Vostro ritorno, durante l'inverno, speriamo che questo libro Vi farà rivivere i giorni felici passati nel paese di Assynt.

Mentre scrivo, i crofter di Assynt vivono giorni storici. La Assynt Crofters' Trust (Associazione dei crofter di Assynt) è riuscita a comperare la proprietà di North Lochinver. Cosi, per la prima volta, i crofter hanno la possibilità di gestire i propri terreni.

La vita in questo paese bellissimo è varia ed animata e speriamo che troverete il tempo per assaporaria.

> Madeline Macphail
> Presidente
> Gruppo Turistico di Assynt

crofting p12

Quinag, an undulating ridge walk

CONTENTS

View across Stoer, the mountains stand one from another in splendid isolation.

INTRODUCTION

'Assynt is a delightful reality at the time of visiting it, while afterwards it fades into a dreamland of stately mountains and lochs studded with water lilies'

Cornhill Magazine 1879

Situated in the far north-west corner of Scotland, amid some of the wildest and most remote scenery anywhere, for those who look, is Assynt.

The name Assynt has several possible derivations. The native Gaelic offers one most in keeping with the shape of the land. 'As agus int', translated literally as 'in and out', contracts conveniently to 'Assint', in obvious reference to the humps and hollows formed by loch and mountains. The early written form was actually 'Asseynkt' as recorded in 1343.

A search through Viking vocabulary will find 'asynt' meaning visible or seen from afar, as the many peaks would be from the Minch, and 'ass-endi' meaning ridge end. Alternatively, a follower of St Columba, Assain, may have left his name with the Picts 200 years before the Norsemen arrived. Most likely though, is the suggestion that the name comes from 'Ass', the Norse word for a rocky place. You can take your pick.

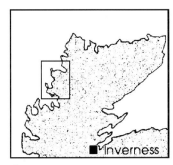

Assynt

At its widest the parish is about 24 miles, east to west, and 21 miles north to south covering some 110,000 acres. The whole area is dominated by the surrounding mountains of Cul Mor, Cul Beag, Stac Pollaidh, Canisp, Suilven, Ben More Assynt, Conival and Quinag (coon-yag).

The communities that grew up here are mostly crofting townships, Elphin is a small inland example, now supplemented, as many are, by crafts and tourism. More often though, the townships are scattered along the coast, like those at Drumbeg, Nedd and Stoer. The population has recovered from a low point of 600 in the late 1950s to well over 1000, but this is still only a third of the number living in Assynt a century ago.

Lochinver is an important fishing port and very much at the heart of Assynt. The village provides a wide range of services for the other smaller communities of the parish. For tourists there are a full range of facilities including information centre, shops, a bank, petrol and accommodation. The Highland Games are held here in August each year. (Other villages surrounding Assynt with a wide range of facilities include Scourie, Achiltibuie and further south the small town of Ullapool).

South of Lochinver, the road passes more crofting townships on the way to Inverkirkaig, the site of an 11th century Culdee religious settlement. The monks were allowed to marry, but their wives lived separately in Badnaban, 'the village of the women or nuns'.

To the north of Lochinver, the coast road winds past some of the most spectacular scenery imaginable. White sandy bays of turquoise waters can be found at Clashnessie and Clachtoll while the views over Eddrachillis Bay defy description. Please note this is a steep and twisting road, frequently single track with passing places, and not suitable for wide or long vehicles. Achmelvich and Stoer Point are separate spurs off this

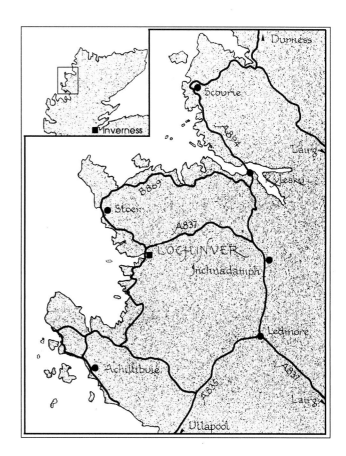

circuit, but both worthy detours. Achmelvich has a magnetic appeal, offering a popular, clean, family-sized beach.

Kylesku marks the northern gateway to Assynt with its award-winning bridge, opened by Her Majesty Queen Elizabeth II in August 1984. The main route south joins the Lochinver road at Skiag Bridge passing Inchnadamph for Lairg or branching back to Elphin.

The climate in Assynt often appears to take no heed of the rest of the country. Here, the weather is controlled by the mountains and the sea on a local basis. The Gulf Stream's influence keeps autumn and winter months relatively mild, snows come and go, but without much persistent frost. In the spring and summer, sea breezes may bathe the coastal districts, but a rainy day inland can often be transformed by taking just a short drive.

The national weather forecasts tend not to take account of the effect Quinag and Suilven have on the winds or clouds, so ask locally. Many who live and work here plan their day-to-day business based on their forecasting knowledge. Be prepared for all weathers; it is changeable, but most of all, enjoy the long summer days.

Something else to prepare for are midges, though only the females bite. Males prefer nectar and rotting plants. Two tips, in addition to using a repellent to avoid attack, relate to midge behaviour; few are active biters in bright daylight and if the wind rises above a stiff breeze, they head for the shelter and warmth of the peat bog. So keep a weather eye for bright, breezy days and groups of male midges.

No small book on Assynt can be all things to all people. This guide is intended to give a flavour of Assynt, past and present, and describe some of the wildlife, places of interest and activities that this corner of Sutherland has to offer. It has been put together by people living in or well connected with Assynt, drawing on their specialised local knowledge.

The proceeds of the sale of this book will be used to promoted tourism within Assynt and to provide better facilities and information for tourists in the future.

Elphin magic

DOWN THROUGH THE CENTURIES *Malcolm Bangor-Jones*

Despite its rugged and barren appearance, Assynt has been settled for many thousands of years. The caves up the valley of the Allt nan Uamh contained hundreds of reindeer antlers thought to have been collected by people not long after the end of the ice-age about 10,000 years ago. By about 5000 BC, Assynt was largely covered by woods of Scots pine and birch and was probably home to small groups of hunters and fishers. From about 3500 BC new peoples brought settled agriculture; the growing of crops and the herding of livestock. These Neolithic people have left little evidence apart from a number of chambered cairns, tombs with burial chambers made of large stone slabs, in the area of better soils between Knockan and Loch Assynt. A bronze axe found near Inchnadamph and the recent discovery of several round houses is all that can presently be dated to the Bronze Age. The climate, however, was becoming colder and wetter and peat growth led to a further decline of local pine forest and the abandonment of some areas. Society was put under a good deal of stress and small forts or duns came to be built. Such defensive structures became widespread during the Iron Age which began about 600 BC.

The earliest forts were constructed with a timber framework which, when burnt, caused the stones forming the core of the walls to melt, a process known as vitrification. The traces of a vitrified fort are to be found on the rocks at Clachtoll. There are also remains of several stone forts along the coast, for example at Ardvar. On the edge of the sea at Clachtoll there is a ruined broch or fort. Its walls have tumbled but the massive lintel stone above the entrance is still in place. Some of these forts may have been re-used during a later period.

Nothing is known about the history of Assynt in the Dark Ages. We may assume, though, that it was part of the kingdom of the Picts and that in time it came under the influence of Gaelic-speaking Scots who had moved north after migrating from Ireland to Argyll in the 5th century. Moreover, it was during this period that missionaries of the Celtic Church brought Christianity to the West Highlands. The way of life, however, was to be rudely shattered by the appearance of Viking raiders towards the end of the eighth century. Many later settled, although the limited number of Norse place-names suggests that their influence was not as strong as in the Northern or Western Isles. Sutherland itself was the south land of the Vikings - literally the southern half of the old province of Caithness - which was held by the Norse Earls of Orkney from the King of Scotland.

The native aristocracy was not wholly exterminated by the Vikings and by the 11th century Gaelic had become the main language. Assynt emerges from this period in the hands of the MacNicols who also held the island of Lewis. The MacNicols did not possess Assynt for more than about 100 years before the lands passed through marriage to Murdoch MacLeod in Harris, a descendant of a Sutherland Viking. His son, Torquil, succeeded to the MacNicol lands and became MacLeod of Lewis, although according to tradition this was after the MacNicols had been wiped out. In 1343 Torquil received a charter of the lands of Assynt from David II in return for the service of a 20-oared Hebridean galley. This was one of several grants of lands made to the west Highland chieftains in an attempt to secure their allegiance to the Scottish crown during the wars of Independence. Early in the 15th century, Assynt was given to a younger son of the MacLeods of Lewis, who became the first of the MacLeods of Assynt.

The family had two strongholds on Loch Assynt; one on an island near the southern shore and the other at Ardvreck not far from the parish church at Inchnadamph. Ardvreck, which dates from the 16th century, was the scene of many incidents in the violent and bloody feuds of the MacLeods. As a small clan, the MacLeods of Assynt were drawn into the quarrels of the MacLeods of Lewis and also the struggles of the Earls of Sutherland and Caithness and the Mackays. The MacLeods then became a target for the Mackenzies, who ousted the clan from Lewis and in the process obtained a right to Assynt. In 1617 Donald Ban MacLeod of Assynt, described by the Government as a lawless Highlander who had committed shameful and barbarous murders, handed over the estate to his eldest son. He managed to evade the course of justice and the family also received help from the Earl of Sutherland's family who were probably eager to keep the Mackenzies out. Despite their difficulties the MacLeods were actively involved in selling cattle, the local fisheries and the manufacture of iron using ore dug from peat bogs.

The ravages of the Civil War brought considerable hardship. The Mackenzies raided Assynt, burning houses and carrying off livestock. Then in 1650 Neil MacLeod of Assynt, a sheriff-depute of the time, captured the Royalist commander, the Marquis of Montrose, after his defeat at the Battle of Carbisdale. Montrose was imprisoned in Ardvreck before being taken to Edinburgh for execution. In the years following the Restoration of a Royalist government, the episode brought Neil a great deal of trouble, including periods of imprisonment in Edinburgh. The Mackenzies took advantage, bought up debts against the estate and in 1672 invaded Assynt. Ardvreck castle surrendered and Neil was forced to flee, losing his charters and only finding sanctuary in Edinburgh. Assynt was acquired by a younger son of the Earl of Seaforth and a number of Mackenzies were settled as tenants.

Unlike the people of Assynt, the Mackenzies were Catholics. They built Calda House, a small mansion house near to Ardvreck, in the mid 1720s. The family, however, ran into financial difficulties and their estate became the subject of a dispute between the Earl of Sutherland and Mackenzie of Seaforth during which Calda House was burnt down by men sent by Seaforth. The bankrupt estate was sold to the Sutherland family in 1757.

Although every farm grew oats and barley, Assynt was renowned for its cattle which were driven to markets in the Lowlands of Scotland and England. The larger farmers, who leased extensive grazings, prospered and built good houses. In the meantime, more and more people were living on the coast. Money earned in the herring fishery, through selling fish or gutting and packing, along with the introduction of the potato, encouraged young people to marry and start families. A fishing station, with sheds for curing and smoking herring, was built at Lochinver in 1775.

The contrast between the interior and the coast of the parish deepened with the introduction of sheep farming. The Sutherland estate had, unlike other northern estates, held back from creating sheep farms. However, the reluctance of the people to enlist in the landlord's regiment, the 93rd Sutherland Highlanders, encouraged the estate to think about a considerable "thinning" of the population. In 1803 the Countess of Sutherland's husband succeeded as Marquis of Stafford and inherited an immense fortune. The family was now extremely rich and able to plan a development programme including the introduction of sheep and the resettlement of people on the coast, where they would be given holdings so small that they would be forced to become fishermen. It was hoped that the Clearances would bring about a vast increase in the landlord's income.

The first Clearances in Assynt took place in 1812 when the Sutherland Estate managers, William Young and Patrick Sellar, reorganised much of the parish into 5 large sheep farms. Between 1812 and 1821 over 160 families were evicted, most of whom were crowded into coastal townships or farms. Resistance to the Clearances was strong and in 1813 there was a riot at Inchnadamph over the appointment of a church minister thought to be favourable to the clearance policy. The plan was not a success, many families left the estate, a local fishing industry never developed on the scale envisaged and the village of Lochinver, founded in 1812, only grew slowly.

Under the leadership of the formidable James Loch, the estate management came to exercise an extraordinarily tight control over people's lives. The cultivation of holdings was encouraged, as was the building of better houses, and the road to Lochinver was completed in 1828. But apart from money earned in the east coast herring fishery or from casual work in the south, people became almost totally depen-

Eadra Chalda, (above) and Kirkton, (below) the ruins remember

dent on the potato. One effect of these difficulties was the growing influence of a very strong evangelical Christianity. Not surprisingly almost everyone joined the Free Church at the time of the great disruption of the established church in 1843.

When the potato crop failed in the late 1840s, there was great suffering. The estate helped by employing people on road building and establishing the plantations around Lochinver and assisted many families to emigrate to Australia. The tenants' holdings, made up of small strips of lands scattered about each farm, were reorganised into individual holdings, or crofts. However, an attempt to clear Knockan and Elphin in 1851 was abandoned after meeting with strong resistance from the crofters - the law officers were stripped and their papers burnt.

For sheep farmers, times could not have been better. A difficult period after the end of the Napoleonic War, when several sheep farmers went bankrupt, gave way to a mid Victorian boom. However, by the 1880's sheep farming was once again facing depression, pastures were eaten out and there was growing competition from the colonies. But the demand for sport was rising - following Queen Victoria's example a Highland season had become very popular - and large areas were cleared of sheep and made over to deer forest or stalking ground.

During the 1880's, crofters in the Highlands took direct action to redress their grievances. After a Royal Commission had reported, an Act was passed giving crofters greater rights. It did not fully address the land question and in Assynt discontent centred on the farm of Clashmore that had been cleared of crofters in 1872 to make way for a model farm. Between 1887 and 1888 the landlord's agents, police and law officers were assaulted, the farm was occupied and the steading was burnt down. The marines were called in to restore order and arrest the ringleaders. Later, large areas of additional grazings were handed over to the crofters.

From the mid-nineteenth century, the population of Assynt continued to fall as young people went south to the cities or abroad in search of greater opportunity. Since the First World War, however, Assynt has experienced change on a greater scale than ever before.

MISTY MEMORIES

Founded in 1775, the fish processing station at Culag marked a significant prelude to the development of Lochinver. John Joseph Bacon from the Isle of Man with a local partner, John Ross, invested £2,000 to build a large curing house and a dwelling house. By 1786 they got into 'vexatious trouble' with customs over some salt and were eager to transfer their four-acre feu, which was bought by Donald Macdonald who also bought the fishing station at Tanera.

At this time the British Fisheries Society was attempting to create new communities in remoter areas but rejected Lochinver as having too little flat land to accommodate a large village. Some 25 years later, at the time Elphin was being created, Lochinver took another step forward, populated as a result of the clearances.

By 1831, Lochinver could be described as having some good houses, shops and several tradesmen, a post office and savings bank - truly established.

SS Claymore, the first ship actually built for David MacBrayne in 1881. He had become a partner when his uncles sold their West Highland steamers to David Hutcheson. Her route was from Glasgow to Stornoway supplying mainland ports like Gairloch, Poolewe, Aultbea, Lochinver and Loch Inchard. She continued in service until 1931 when, having been reprieved for a year, she was sold for scrap for £75.

The 'Steamer' called at Lochinver until 1947. In early times this was an important day when all horses, carts and owners gathered at the pier. It usually led to convivial meetings at the Culag - no driving licences were required for horse and cart and there were no breathalysers.

1929 A new bus for the Lochinver - Invershin Motor Co.

At this time the road was little more than a dirt track, grass usually grew up the middle. It was not until the 1960s that it improved to a good single track!

Fondly remembered, the Kylesku ferry did charge a princely 6s 0d (when 30p was a lot of money) for a motor car up to 10 h.p. before being operated by the council as a free service.

LIFE TODAY *Isobel MacPhail, Roddy MacLeod, Alex Dickson, Fiona MacAulay, Kenny Mackenzie*

What is crofting?

Crofting is a land-based activity and, above all, a distinctive way of life. Crofters complement seasonal agricultural tasks with a variety of other activities such as fish farming, building and construction, B&B, self-catering accommodation and hotel work, fishing and related industries, employment with the Regional Council or in a range of other local shops or businesses.

A croft comprises an individual plot of land of about 5 acres and a share in the common grazings. The crofter is the tenant. Crofts are organised in townships, managed communally by each township's elected grazings committee. At different times of the year crofters from each township often come together to gather their sheep for clipping and dipping.

In the wake of the hardships of the Clearances and the outcry and uprisings of the Crofters' Wars, the crofting system's legal and administrative framework was established by Act of Parliament in 1866. The Act brought crofters security of tenure and a right to fair rents. The land around the coast on which the people settled after being cleared was poor, poor land - but hard won land for all that.

On this land the crofters struggled to grow enough oats, barley, vegetables and winter feed to keep their families and stock. Today most of the croft land in Assynt provides grazing for sheep and some cattle, but the layout of the crofts remains largely as it was a century ago. Crofting is characterised by low-intensity agricultural practices that, in recent years, have found favour with the RSPB and other agencies working to conserve the natural environment.

Over the years the crofting system has proved vital in anchoring communities in the remoter corners of the Highlands and Islands all the year round. The social and cultural aspects of crofting and the diverse lifestyles it supports are as crucial as its value as a low-intensity landuse. To be a crofter in Assynt is to be part of an active community for whom the culture of Gaeldom is very much a lived and cherished thing.

One of the issues the 1886 crofting Act failed to tackle was the crofters' demand that the land be returned to the people. But in 1992 the crofters of Assynt took on this issue themselves ...

* Forme d'agriculture caractéristique des Highlands. Le croft est une petite parcelle de terre assortie du droit de laisser pâitre un certain nombre de têtes de bétail sur les pâturages communs, et d'extraire la tourbe des tourbières communes, pour se chauffer. Le crofter est locataire de ses terres, qui dépendent le plus souvent d'un grand domaine.

* "Crofting" ist eine Landwirtschaftsform, die für das schottische Hochland typisch ist. Beim "Crofter" handelt es sich um einen Kleinbauer, der das Recht hat, eine bestimmte Anzahl Vieh auf dem gemeinsamen Weideland zu halten und Torf für den eigenen Kamin im gemeindeeigenen Moor zu stechen. Die "Crofters" sind Pächter, und die meisten "Crofts" gehören zu großen Ländereien.

* Tipo de explotación agrícola propia de las Tierras Altas de Escocia. El croft es una pequeña parcela de tierra a la que el campesino puede llevar a pastar un número determinado de animales en pastos compartidos y en la que extrae, de las turberas comunales, la turba necesaria para calentar su casa. Los crofters arriendan estas tierras que, por lo general, se encuentran en grandes fincas.

* Tipo di agricoltura caratteristica delle Highlands. Il croft è un piccolo terreno con il diritto di pascolo per del bestiame sulla pastura commune e di estrarre torba per il camino dalle torbiere comunali. Il crofter è locatario dei suoi terreni, che generalmente appartengono a grandi proprietà terriere.

HARD WON LAND, FOR ALL THAT

North Assynt Estate

On 8th December 1992 the Assynt Crofters Trust won an historic victory, gaining the title to the land on which they live and work, bringing their land into community ownership.

In the spring of 1992 the North Lochinver Estate, which runs from Achmelvich to Loch Nedd was put up for sale in several small lots. For people living there the prospect of a multiplicity of disinterested or negligent landlords loomed large.

At a public meeting the crofters unanimously resolved to mount a campaign to buy the land and secure the future for them-

selves and younger generations, through the control of their own resources. Inspiration came from the struggles of the past to hold onto this hard won land and also from the widespread support which the campaign gained. And so, the Assynt Crofters Trust was formed by the Estate's crofters - all with equal voting rights in the Trust.

In December 1992 history had turned full circle when the Assynt Crofters were able to purchase the land, and as the local MP said, 'lit a beacon throughout Scotland'. A beacon of hope for a more secure future and a say in that future!

Gaelic

It is remarkable to find that a majority of the people in Assynt were bilingual around the 1920s. Prior to this, Gaelic had held the upper hand but then teachers from the south drove the language from the classroom and punished its use in the playground. As the population declined, the Gaelic speakers became fewer and older with a possibility that the language could die with them.

Now the population is gradually increasing again and many people are taking an interest in life as part of this formally gael community. Adults are taking up the language in evening classes and the children are going to croileagan - Gaelic playgroup. The wheel has turned full circle.

As a language that has always been spoken more than written, the derivation and spelling of place names has always been difficult. In Assynt, the influence of Norse words, like sula - a pillar - when mixed with the Gaelic beinn leads to the more complex origin of Suilven.

Pronunciation

Bh or Mh equals V
Cn equals Kr
-aidh equals y as in my
-idh equals y as in duty

Some Gaelic words commonly found in place names

Ach: A mound or bank
Achadh: A field, plain or meadow
Allt: A burn or stream; other forms used are alt, ault, ald, auld
Ard: A height or promontory; another form is aird
Bad: A place, sometimes a clump or thicket
Bal (baile): A farm settlement or village
Beag: Little
Beinn: A mountain; other forms are ben, bheinn
Eilean: Island
Inver (inbhir): Rivermouth
Kin (ceann): The head - of a loch etc.
Mor: Large

A', Am, An t- and Na mean 'the'
A', An t-, Na, Nan and Nam mean 'of the'

Place name meanings

Achadh na carnin	The field of cairns (heaps of stones)
Achmelvich	Field of the sand dunes
Alltan na Bradhan	Burn of steep braes
Ardroe	High headland
Ardvar	High point
Ardvreck	Speckled point
Altnacealgach	Burn of the deceivers
Baddidarach	A clump of oaks
Badnaban	Place of women
Balchladich	Village by the shore
Brackloch	Place of fallen trees or the trout loch
Clachtoll	Stone with a hole
Clashmore	Big gully
Clashnessie	Valley of the waterfall
Culag	Nook, recess
Culkein	Behind the headland
Drumbeg	Little ridge
Elphin	White stone
Inchnadamph	Pasture of the ox or stag
Inverkirkaig	The kirk at the mouth of the river
Knockan	Hillock
Kylesku	Narrow channel
Ledmore	Steep slope
Ledbeg	Little slope
Lochinver	Loch of the estuary
Nedd	The nest
Oldany	River of tidal flats
Stoer	Sea stack
Strathan	Little valley
Stronchrubie	Twisted nose
Torbreck	Speckled hillock

Mountains

Beinn Gharbh	Rough mountain
Beinn Ghoblach	Forked mountain
Beinn Uidhe	Journey mountain
Ben More Assynt	Assynt's big mountain
Cromalt	Curved mountain
Cul Beag	Small back
Cul Mor	Big back
Glas Bheinn	Grey mountain
Quinag	Milking-pail
Sail Gharbh	Rough heel
Sail Gorm	Blueish-green heel
Sail Liath	Grey heel
Stac Pollaidh	Steep hill of the peat bog

Lochs

Loch an Arbhair	The corn loch
Loch Beannach	The forked loch
Loch Borralan	Loch of the waves
Cam Loch	Crooked or bent loch
Loch a Chairn Bhain	Loch of the white cairns
Loch a Choin	The loch of the dog

Loch Crocach	Branch loch
Loch na Claise	The loch of the hollow
Loch na Creige Leithe	The loch of the grey rock
Loch Dubh	Black loch
Loch Fada	The long loch
Fionn Loch	The white loch
Loch na Gainmhich	Sandy loch
Loch na Gobhar	The loch of the goats
Loch an Leothard	The loch of the steep hill
Loch nan Lub	The loch of the bends
Loch Neil Bhain	Fair Neil's loch
Loch Poll	The pool or pond

> When asked if there was a word, equivalent to the Spanish mañana, the old Gaelic speaker said "No-o-o, nothing with quite the same degree of urgency"

Fishing

At the beginning of this century the fishing industry was limited to small boats line-fishing, and herring fishing in season. Even back in those days these small boats landed herring to Klondykers - German Klondykers anchored at Kylesku. These small boats made Lochinver a recognised port and consigned their fish to markets in Billingsgate, Hull and Grimsby via bus to Invershin and on by rail. They even made their own fish-boxes.

One local boat graduated to seine-netting and before long boats from Helmsdale, Buckie, Banff, Macduff, Lossiemouth, Whitehills and Wick had moved in and based themselves at Lochinver. The crews lived on board, going home by road at weekends, whenever possible.

Lochinver, white painted cottages lead to the harbour

market with offices, a finger jetty and a new breakwater, not to mention the associated roadworks and the creation of new land for further development.

Although there has been a downturn in the fishing industry recently, Lochinver has thrived because of the activities of a fleet of large French trawlers fishing beyond the continental shelf, and bringing in hitherto unknown fish. They have based themselves at the port, taking over the old fish market and adding some very welcome employment.

Tourism

In the pre-war years tourism in Assynt was confined, mainly, to the 'well-to-do'. They came for the fishing and stalking and stayed in the few hotels or estate houses in the area.

In the 50s, with the advent of electric power and mains water to many of the croft houses, it became possible to offer bed and breakfast facilities for the adventurous traveller. The 60s brought a real growth in car ownership in Britain and the coming of the caravan. This gave the opportunity, as it still does today, for a family to have a relatively cheap holiday and the freedom to explore the further reaches of Scotland.

By the early 70s, this growth had accelerated until the area reached saturation level at the height of each

Lochinver became a thriving port and with an increase in shell-fishing as well, improvement of the port facilities became necessary. The first major extension was opened in July 1969 where the ice-plant now stands. But fish were still sold in the open, and it was not until September 1974 that a covered fish market was opened on a second pier extension.

The acquisition by Highland Regional Council of land round the Culag Hotel made further expansion possible and in September 1992 a sizeable new development was opened incorporating a pier extension, a new larger fish summer. The main road into Assynt from the South was by this time upgraded to twin track and the parish had become even more attractive to motorists.

However, around this time, the numbers visiting Assynt peaked as many people turned to cheap European package holidays for their summer vacation. The decline in the number of visitors was relatively short-lived and this has been reversed steadily through the 80s and 90s.

The reasons for this growth in the last twenty years have been: the greater number of people taking more than one vacation per year, a substantial rise in the volume of European visitors and a large increase in the amount of self-catering accommodation available.

Tourists to Assynt now have a wide choice of quality accommodation available to them from hotels, guest houses, bed and breakfast, self-catering, camping or hostelling.

Crafts

The area has never had an indigenous craft industry such as those found on Lewis or Shetland and, in the main, is more individual. A weaver, knitter, or painter might well pursue another means of support in tandem with the craft work.

The outstanding exception to this has been the growth of Highland Stoneware. The pottery was started in 1974 and is now a substantial employer in Lochinver. They also have a retail shop in Ullapool and export their earthenware all around the world.

Fish farming

Fish farming began experimentally in this area in the 1970's. Salmon farming has now grown to be a multi-million pound industry employing a significant number of local people. The industry's success has helped stabilise the local population and has brought young people to the area, resulting in house-building programmes, schools being kept open and local businesses being supported.

Around Assynt, visitors will notice collections of circular tanks - these are freshwater hatcheries, the first stage in the salmon's cycle. Here the eggs are hatched and the young fry grow to become smolts. These are transferred to the sea cages in May, often using helicopters to transport them in large buckets from the hatchery.

Sea cages are situated in the many sheltered lochs up and down the west coast, taking advantage of the clear unpolluted waters. The salmon are raised in these cages and harvested either as grilse after 1 year or salmon after 2 years. Some are retained as brood stock, and when mature (some 10 kgs in weight) their eggs will be returned to the hatchery to start the cycle again.

Salmon farming has been one of the success stories in the development and regeneration of the Highlands. The visitor will find that many of the farms sell fresh and smoked local salmon - bon appétit!

Creag Liath

THE GREAT OUTDOORS *Tom Strang, Stuart McClelland*

Hill-walking

Hill-walking takes on a new dimension here. There are few proper paths and fewer signposts - a rare occurrence in view of the growing compulsion to build cairns of stone in unlikely and usually unnecessary places on mountainsides. You can still walk here all day and not see another soul. For the more adventurous, the ridges offer a delightful prospect of scrambling over ledges and pinnacles. For rock climbers, there is still the chance to put up a new line in hidden corners just over the skyline. In winter the mountains of Assynt, like those of other parts of the Highlands, have to be treated with proper respect to be enjoyed in safety. Waterproof clothing and suitable footwear are essential at all times.

Conival and Ben More Assynt, the highest summits in the area, are both Munros. Each year, hordes of hill walkers make the pilgrimage eager to tick them off their list. Corbett bagging is just as popular so Quinag, Cul Mor, Cul Beag and others are not left to feel ignored.

The Assynt Mountain Rescue Team's booklet, **"Making more of Assynt"**, details several of these walks and climbs. Another essential reference, the Ordnance Survey Landranger sheet 15 for Loch Assynt and the surrounding area, details the paths and peat tracks.

On Suilven

Going Underground

Caves are formed by the solvent effect of weak acids in rainwater acting on rocks that are rich in calcium carbonate. Water percolates through the cracks and fissures of such rocks, eventually enlarging them into caverns and passageways. These should be entered only by those who are properly equipped and trained. These safety precautions cannot be over-stressed: the flooding hazard is very pronounced as all areas have high rainfall. Caving in Scotland is not be undertaken lightly.

Some of the most impressive caving areas are to be found in Assynt. Along the valley of the River Traligill, east of Inchnadamph, a number of very prominent cave entrances can be examined by the interested walker, although few of these are accessible to the casual visitor. The famous Bone Caves are located 1.25 miles up the valley of the Allt nan Uamh, at the base of a prominent crag. These caves are one of the earliest archaeological sites in Scotland, with remains dated to 8000 BC; further digging is prohibited without permission from the Nature Conservancy Council.

The Valley of the Trolls

A walk along the prettiest limestone valley in Scotland, forming part of the Inchnadamph National Nature Reserve. The walk is 4.5 miles long and although relatively easy, care must be taken to follow directions and take note of warnings. Time: allow 4 to 5 hours as there is a lot to see.

Drive along the A837 to Inchnadamph, at the east end of Loch Assynt. Cars can be left immediately on the north side of the road bridge over the River Traligill (from the Norse, Troll meaning giant and gill meaning ravine), near the gated private road that parallels the river upstream. Sturdy boots or shoes, with support for the ankle, are necessary for walking in the area as the ground is rugged. A waterproof cagoule and over-trousers are also useful - the Assynt mountains are among the wettest in the country, and the local weather can be very changeable.

There are few access restrictions in this area, but during the main stalking season from August to October, it may be as well to check with the keeper at Stronchrubie or Assynt Estate Office, Lochinver.

Walk up the private road, making sure you leave all gates as you find them. The road soon deteriorates into a wide gravel track; follow it for about half a mile to where it crosses the Allt Poll an Droighinn. By taking a short detour you can follow alongside this tributary stream to the north-west to the edge of the limestone outcrop. The deeply incised stream tumbles, by way of two pretty waterfalls, Eas na Saighe Caime, from the adjoining quartzite. There are no paths to the falls, but as long as you watch your footing, the heather poses few problems. It is best to follow the southern side of the stream as it is easier to join the track by following the fence from the waterfalls.

Continue along the stony track on to and beyond Glenbain Cottage - the wide track breaks to the right and peters out. Instead branch left, keeping the drystone wall on your right. The footpath you follow eventually leads you past a small conifer plantation to the River Traligill. Although winter floods periodically sweep away the wooden bridge here, it is fairly easy to cross using the boulders that lie on its bed. A prominent flat-topped knoll, Cnoc nan Uamh (hill of the caves), to the south-east, is the next objective. A number of narrow footpaths will lead you there, or you can invent your own route, meandering among the dry channels and peat-filled depressions so characteristic of limestone areas.

On reaching the hill you will encounter three large cave entrances. The easternmost, Uamhan Tartair (cave of the roaring), appears to be an enclosed chamber, but by scrambling under an overhang you can enter a large stream passage. A light is necessary, NO ONE BUT EXPERIENCED CAVERS SHOULD ATTEMPT TO ENTER THESE CAVES AND ALL VISITORS SHOULD EXERCISE EXTREME CAUTION. The other entrances are a large open pothole (keep away from the edge, which is prone to crumble) and Uamh an Uisge (cave of the water), where the cave stream plunges ferociously down a thrust plane, to emerge much further down the valley. Around the contour of the hill, a dry stream bed can be followed up to a dry waterfall that intersects part of an old cave, Uamh Caillich Peireag.

The return leg of the walk follows the dry bed of the Allt a' Bhealaich burn, which is rarely full of water. On reaching the River Traligill once again, turn left to follow the river to where it sinks underground at Lower Traligill Cave. Down-valley of the cave, the stream bed is usually dry, except after a few days of rain. Drainage water here follows a subterranean course below the prominent cliff that forms the left bank. The right bank is an inclined fault plane, along which the rocks must have been thrust by the earth's movements millions of years ago. In places this thrust plane surface is covered with strange patterns. These patterns are a characteristic feature of weathered limestone surfaces.

The Traligill eventually reappears from beneath what is usually a dry waterfall at Traligill Rising. From here, you can either regain the footpath back to Glenbain by crossing the degraded drystone dykes, or continue to follow the Traligill downstream along the top of a narrow gorge. At all times, keep to the northern bank. Return via the stony track, before the scattered cottages opposite the Inchnadamph Hotel.

Angling

Assynt is studded with lochs. The lochs vary tremendously in shape and size, but they have one factor in common - wild brown trout. This is the angler's paradise, long renowned for fine sport in unparalleled conditions. Many of the best known waters - Urigill, Borralan, Veyatie, Fionn and The Cam Loch (the names a mixture of Norse and Gaelic) - lie in the southern corner of Assynt around the crofting communities of Knockan and Elphin.

Here trout rise freely to fly, and fight like fish twice their weight. The chance of landing a big fish is always there; monsters of up to 12 lb. have been recorded over the years. Further north around Lochinver, Drumbeg and the Stoer peninsula, the Assynt Angling Club and North Assynt Estate operate on more than 30 smaller lochs of similar high quality. Indeed, around this part of Assynt there is more water to negotiate inland than there is dry land.

Loch Assynt, the largest extent of fresh water, cuts across the very centre of the district, stretching six miles westwards from Inchnadamph towards Lochinver, with an outlet to the sea via the River Inver itself. This has superb situations and enjoys magnificent sunsets, with the towering peak of Quinag along its northern shoreline and the stark ruined keep of Ardvreck Castle, with its memories and ghosts, silhouetted on its grassy peninsula in the foreground. Large 'brownies' and ferox are caught here; with sea trout and salmon an added bonus.

Few areas in Scotland offer the visiting angler such a diversity of easily accessible, excellent sport. Shimmering roadside waters, where it is possible to step almost straight from the car into a boat; remote, distant mountain lochs and lochans that take hours to reach but give a lifetime's pleasure once there. This is a land where game-fishing dreams come true, and each day brings ever-increasing contentment.

Borralan is the ideal place for a relaxing day's sport. Trout average 6 to 8 oz and baskets of 30 or more fish are common. That much over-worked angling phrase, 'free-rising', really does apply to Borralan, and although the fish are quite small, they fight like demons.

South from Borralan is another loch, Loch Urigill, which is also full of free-rising fish, but on Urigill there is always the chance of a better trout and fish of up to 2 lb are sometimes caught. Both these waters have a mayfly hatch in late June - sport is then fast and furious.

The tiny village of Elphin, on the A835 south from Ledmore Junction, is the starting point for fishing The Cam Loch (the crooked loch) and long, windy Veyatie. Cam Loch trout average 8 to 12 oz and rise to all the standard patterns of Scottish loch flies; but the loch is very deep and contains ferox, cannibal trout that grow to a great size. It is best to fish for them using the old Scottish method of trolling.

The Cam Loch cascades seawards through Veyatie, a long wind-tunnel of a loch, where the best sport is at the east end. Trout on Veyatie average 10 oz and large baskets are the rule rather than the exception. But there are much larger fish; one of 9lb was landed recently, close to the narrow rock bar that separates Veyatie from Loch a' Mhadail on the south shore.

Follow Veyatie north-westwards and you arrive at one of Assynt's finest and most prolific waters, Fionn Loch. In fact, access is from Inverkirkaig, south from Lochinver, and the four-mile track out to Fionn follows the north bank of the Kirkaig River past deep, silent pools where salmon lie.

Salmon enter the river in March, but the main run does not start until July. The end of the road for Kirkaig salmon is in Falls Pool, below a dramatic impassable 60 foot high waterfall. A few minutes after leaving Falls Pool you arrive at Fionn Loch, guarded northwards by the towering heights of Caisteal Liath, (the grey castle), the highest point of Suilven.

Fionn is a long straggling loch with myriad bays and corners, collecting together waters from thousands of acres

before plunging seawards down Kirkaig River. Brown trout average 8 to 12 oz, but fish of over 3 lb are often caught.

North from Fionn, near Inchnadamph, Loch Assynt offers superb sport for visiting anglers; wonderful baskets of hard-fighting small brown trout and fine doughty salmon. More than 50 salmon and grilse are taken each year, and boats are readily available from the Inchnadamph Hotel.

Loch na Creige Leithe, typical of the North Assynt Estate

The diminutive Loch Awe, south of Assynt, also contains a few salmon, as well as hundreds of brown trout; what greater pleasure can there be than landing a sparkling grilse on a size 14 Pennel on a trout rod?

But to some, of all the fishing wonders of Assynt, the best lie out in the hills and mountains, on the dozens of lochs managed by the Assynt Angling Club and North Assynt Estate. Details of permits and prices are available from the Tourist Information Centre.

Fishing Season
Salmon: March until October (best from July onwards).
Trout:　March until September (best during late June / July and September).

Sea Fishing

The waters off the Assynt coast offer the serious sea angler great opportunities for specimen hunting. But for the visitor just wanting a spot of fun fishing there are many boats that will take you out for a few hour's enjoyment. Most of the skippers will provide bait and basic fishing tackle. Conveniently, you are fishing close to shore here but it is often worth using bigger bait than usual. There is a good variety of fish; cod, ling, wrasse or, off Handa, haddock, a real bonus for the rod fisherman. The rocky gullies and forests of kelp are always home to pollack, a powerful fish and great sport on light tackle.

Over the years, dedicated sea anglers have landed some large fish. Skate, shark and halibut have all been caught though they do require persistence and dedication to find.

Safety!

Please ensure that you are properly equipped and remain alert to the safety of your own party (and those who might have to rescue you) whether at sea or beside the most tranquil looking lochan.

ROCKS OF AGES *Chris Pellant*

The landscape of the Lewisian Gneiss is a low uneven one with knobbly hills and irregular valleys. It rises from sea level to a few hundred feet and has been extensively altered in past ice-ages, scoured to produce numerous freshwater lochs and leaving the bays and inlets studded with islands. Along the coast, the magnificent shapes and terraces of the relict Torridonian sandstone mountains with their bare weather-resistant eastern quartzite slopes and tops contrast sharply with welcoming green swards and limestone pavements of Inchnadamph.

Assynt and the surrounding area were first surveyed in detail by the Geological Survey officers Peach, Horne, Clough and Hinxman in the early years of this century. Their report published in 1907 is a classic. Their work has since been revised, but the geological map currently available owes much to these pioneers. A memorial to them is situated near the head of Loch Assynt across the road from the Inchnadamph hotel.

The oldest rock formation, which rests below the others (except where faulting has complicated things), is called the Lewisian Complex, after the Outer Hebridean island where it is abundant. This complex is a fragment of the earth's original continental crust over 2,500 million years old. In the distant past this part of Scotland was joined onto Canada and Greenland, before the Atlantic Ocean formed.

Rocks belonging to the Lewisian are varied, but the typical material is a grey, banded metamorphic rock called gneiss. (Metamorphic rocks are those which have been significantly altered by processes within the Earth's crust.) Banding is caused by the separation of light and dark minerals during the intense pressure and temperature conditions of metamorphism. Before being gneiss these rocks could have been granite, basalt lava or even sediments such as sandstone. A typical fragment of Assynt gneiss contains quite large crystals, many of which glint in the light. The paler bands contain much quartz, a hard, grey mineral that cannot be scratched with a penknife blade, and the darker bands may have much shiny, soft, black mica (scratchable with a finger nail) or hornblende in them.

Long after the Lewisian gneiss had been formed, deep in the Earth's crust, a mountainous area existed roughly where the Outer Hebrides are today. Huge rivers flowed to the East into what is now Assynt, bringing with them sand, gravel and silt; sediment formed from the erosion of the older Lewisian rocks. The famous Assynt mountains such as Suilven and Quinag are largely made of this sediment. It is typically a brown or pinkish-brown sandstone with frag-

Gneiss, formed by intense heat and pressure

ments of grey quartz and a pink, hard, shiny mineral called feldspar.

Originally the whole region was beneath many thousands of feet of Torridonian strata and the isolated mountains are mere fragments of this, left by flukes of weathering and erosion.

Many of the best coastal features in Assynt are to be found where the sandstones reach the sea. The high, dan-gerous cliffs at Stoer Point, where the rock has weathered into ledges favoured by nesting sea birds, are of the rusty sandstone (as are the cliffs of Handa island), and in places erosion has opened up large caves which collapse into arches as at Culkein. Fine caves are to be found around Stoer Head and a collapsed arch occurs at Clachtoll. The famous Old Man of Stoer and other coastal stacks in that area are the result of the continued erosion of arches.

The summits of many of the Assynt hills are capped with silvery rock called quartzite. The slopes of Glas Bheinn on the east of the pass over to Kylesku are made of this, pro-ducing an almost barren landscape. Farther south summits such as Cul Mor are made of quartzite and there are a few fragments of the rock on Suilven's summit. This quartzite was formed in shallow water about 570 million years ago, as the sea came in over the solidified Torridonian sands. Though quartzite is a very hard rock, it is not immune to the processes of glaciation and the great corrie in the north face of Glas Bheinn is cut into this rock.

For those interested in fossils the layers above the quartzite are of great interest because they contain frag-ments of fossil trilobites. These marine creatures, related to modern shrimps and crabs, lived in and on the muddy Cambrian sea bed. They are not easy to find, but the small quarry at Loch Awe often yields specimens. The trilobite found here occurs in Scotland and nowhere else in

Glencoul, the best view of a thrust fault in the British Isles

Britain, yet it is found in North America - further evidence of the link between these areas in the distant past.

The youngest rocks in Assynt, apart from the glacial deposits, are the limestones, a mere 500 million, or so years old. In the valley of the Traligill and at the Allt nan Uamh the limestone has been weathered and eroded into underground river systems and caves, not unlike those to be found in the much younger limestones of the English Pennine dales. Near Ledmore this limestone has been turned into marble of very good quality and a new quarry has recently been opened up just to the east of the road.

Perhaps the most spectacular geological feature is the thrust fault at Loch Glencoul. On the hillside to the north-east of this deep sea loch, the Glencoul thrust displays ancient Lewisian rocks above younger Cambrian strata. Views of this can be had from the road near Unapool. A thrust fault is a large scale dislocation of rocks causing one mass to be pushed over another.

RICH TAPESTRIES OF PLANTS AND ANIMALS *Ian Evans*

Washed by the warm waters of the Gulf Stream and about as far north as possible for mainland Scotland, Assynt has a better claim than most parts of the British Isles to a unique assemblage of plants and animals. The variety is seen through a range of habitats.

The Coast

Sheltered rocky parts of the coast at low tide are a good place to start. Washing around on the lowest parts of the shore are huge fronds of Kelp, the largest of the brown seaweeds. Above the Kelp are successive bands of other brown seaweeds, from Bladder Wrack, which pops when you tread on it, through to the small slippery Channelled Wrack. In more exposed areas, bands of blue Mussels give way to a crunchy band of tiny white Barnacles. Above all of them, the seashore rocks at or above high tide level are painted with the black, white and orange of maritime Lichens.

Spray splashed sea cliffs often bear the hoary coat of another large grey lichen known as Sea Ivory. Crevices on the exposed coasts are the home of tough shiny green fronds of a fern, Sea Spleenwort. Hanging to the vertical rock faces, out of reach of the sheep that will risk their lives for a succulent bite, are the fleshy rosettes of Rose Root, white-flowered Sea Campion and compact tussocks of the aptly named Sea Pink or Thrift.

Quiet inlets on the coast are a good place to look out for Grey Seals bobbing in the surf or hauled out in the sun or on rocky skerries. If you are fortunate you may catch sight of an Otter adding assorted sea-food to its more usual diet of freshwater fish. The patient sea watcher may be rewarded with views of a passing school of Dolphins, Porpoises or even a Minke whale in the summer months.

Assynt's beautiful sandy bays at Achmelvich, Clachtoll and Clashnessie also have their treasures. The tiny pink shelled Thin Tellin and other bivalves share the strandline with delicate red seaweeds washed off the rocks and washed up Common and Compass Jellyfish. Few plants can survive moving sand, but the neat four-square stems of Sea Purslane can grow on dunes stabilised by Marram Grass. As the dunes age they acquire a rich flora including Bird's Foot Trefoil, Frog Orchid and the cream or purplish flowered Autumn Gentians. Caterpillars of Common Blue butterflies and day-flying Six-spot Burnet moths feed on the trefoil.

On rocky crags, often within sight of the sea, grow two of Assynt's specialities. The pale green hairy rosettes of Pyramidal Bugle like areas of bare soil on sunny slopes, often where heather has been burned in previous years. They throw mauve-tinged spikes of flowers early in the

Seals

A knowing look from a grey seal or an inquisitive glance from the smaller common seal, but how do you tell the difference? Look at the head bobbing in front of you - the roman nose with parallel nostrils distinguishes the grey seal from the more dog-like head of the common seal whose nostrils meet in a V-shape. Both can dive to 50m or more for up to half an hour, but these fishing trips are more likely to last just a few minutes.

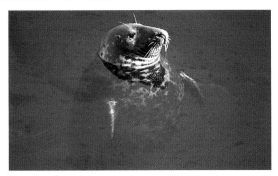

Grey seal

Common seals gather in large groups during the spring. They have their pups in June and breed again at a few favourite spots. Often they can be seen from the bridge at Kylesku. The grey seals must find secluded islands for their breeding season in October as their youngsters are more vulnerable, until they are able to swim at three weeks old.

Though the males mature in about six years, it may take ten years for them to gain a place in the breeding group. The harems are made up of age-ing bulls and females that are at least three years old. The common seals can live to an age of thirty and grey seals may reach thirty-five or more.

Common seal

Top left: Sea rocket - a rare splash of colour in the strandline
Middle left: The rare broad-leaved helleborine
Left: Insect trapping sundew

Above: Lily studded waters abound

summer. Trusses of the purple-veined white flowers of Bitter Vetch hang from vertical faces, where the sheep cannot get at them.

Woodland

Travelling on the coast road from Inverkirkaig round to Kylesku a surprising amount of woodland is seen. These woods are composed of the Birch and Rowan found throughout much of the Highlands, along with several extensive areas of ancient Hazel in sheltered valleys. Other kinds of tree scattered through these woodlands include Sessile Oak, Wych Elm and Aspen with its flaming yellow autumn colours.

In spring the rocky floors of these woodlands are studded with clumps of Primroses and, a little later, Bluebells reflect the colour of the sky (on a good day)! Among them the less common Wild Garlic, Sweet Woodruff and orchids such as the Broad-leaved and Narrow-leaved Helleborines can be found. In the damper areas, boulders up to the size of houses are covered with mosses and ferns, the latter ranging in size from the huge tussocks of Golden-Scaled Male Fern to the tiny crowded fronds of Wilson's Filmy Fern.

In autumn the woodlands are brightened by the reds, browns, yellows and whites of a wide assortment of mushrooms and toadstools, especially those associated with birch, like Penny Buns or Ceps, the white spotted red caps of Fly Agaric and the bright orange edible Chanterelles. As the bracken dies down, the activities of the resident Badger population become obvious. Their setts are usually located in tumbled boulder scree from which they emerge at night to feed. The woodland floor is peppered with holes dug in search of bulbs or worms.

Another creature of the gloaming is the Pine Marten, which raids soft fruit from gardens (they are even partial to raspberry jam sandwiches)! Roe Deer, the smallest of the two native species, are most often seen in the wooded areas, moving quietly and unseen for most of the year but becoming a little more noisy at the rut when the short sharp bark of the bucks may be heard at night. Evening is also a time when bats may be seen chasing moths and other insects over woodland where nearby houses or sheds provide safe roosts and hibernation sites; pipistrelles are the commoner but Long-eared Bats also occur.

The most conspicuous of the day-flying woodland insects are large Longhorn Beetles, whose grubs tunnel in old timber, but you may catch a glimpse of a brilliant blue and black dragonfly, the Azure Hawker, which hunts the edge of woodlands and is confined in Britain to this part of Scotland.

Water

Water is the essence of the interior of this region. There are over 200 lochs and lochans interconnected and draining eventually to the sea by fast flowing burns. The higher ones often look rather dour, plant-life being limited to the pale blue flowers of Water Lobelia, perhaps with a few leaves of Bog Bean in silty places. The sparse marginal vegetation may be the result of exposure, but more often that of grazing, as shown by the lush growth on many of the islands in the lochs. Bordering such islands are often huge clumps of Royal Fern. However lifeless they appear almost all lochs contain Brown Trout and the discerning fisherman matches his flies to the abundant hatches of Mayflies and Stoneflies that occur on warm sunny days.

Insects hatching from the loch and surrounding vegetation provide ample food for the colourful variety of damsel and dragon flies, seen at their best in sheltered bays on calm days. They range in size from the Common Blue, Blue-tailed, Large Red and Emerald Damselflies, through to the larger bodied Highland and Black Darters, the Broad-bodied Four-spotted Chaser, with yellow patches at the base of its wings, to the magnificent Golden-ringed Hawker, which is often seen clinging to heather stems on cold wet days.

Frogs and Toads find ample breeding sites in the small lochans and pools, especially the richer ones with Bulrush and White Water Lilies nearer the coast, although frogs may be found high on the hills in summer. Well-camouflaged Palmate Newts lurk in shallow pools.

Moorland

Drier areas of moorland are dominated by dwarf shrubs, particularly Heather or Ling, at its most colourful in August, when in full flower. Scattered through the heather in the driest parts are the deep crimson flowers of Bell Heather and the pink bells that later turn to the blue-black fruits of Bilberry. A variety of other flowers are found in grassy areas, including the four-petalled yellow flowers of Tormentil and slender St John's-wort.

Wetter moorland areas are spectacular in June when carpeted with the white tasselled seedheads of Cotton Grass. In autumn the rusty brown Deer Grass combines with the yellow of dying leaves of Purple Moor-grass and the red of Cotton Grass to turn the hillsides a lovely foxy colour. In the red, yellow or green tussocks of Bogmoss which enliven the wetter areas the sticky-leafed Sundews and the starfish-like rosettes of Butterwort and the rarer Pale Butterwort may be found. These plants supplement the meagre nutrients available where they live with a diet of insects trapped by their leaves.

Scattered across the moorland, conspicuous pink flowering heads of the Heath Spotted and Fragrant Orchids are

Moss campion flowers from May to August

Eye-catching mountain avens

Orchids - add colour from May

Autumn is the fungi season

Holly fern, typically tucked away

Common blue butterfly

Red deer

With thousands of truly wild red deer parading across the open moors they are an increasingly common sight. Inchnadamph literally means feeding ground of the stag, which is worth remembering when driving at night - no zebra crossing here!

Red deer today are smaller than their ancestors. They moved into Scotland with the spreading forests when the Ice Age came to an end 10,000 years ago. Wolves and lynx used to prey on the abundant herds, keeping the population in check but now the only natural predators of weak calves are the fox and golden eagle. Unfortunately, they are now out of balance with the food supply and are damaging their own habitat.

Red deer are sociable animals, the herds are not just random gatherings. For ten months a year the sexes remain separate; the hinds in large family groups, the stags roam together more loosely. A group of hinds consists of the dominant female, her mature daughters and all their dependant offspring of both sexes. The group may contain 10-30 members.

The calves are usually born in early June. A hind will stay with her dappled calf through the first day then leave the youngster to sit hidden in the heather or bracken for a few days, returning to feed it three times a day.

By the end of September the rutting stags roar to warn others away from their territory and herd their harem.

seen with, in stony areas, the uncommon Small White Orchid. Rather more difficult to find are the tiny stems of Lesser Twayblade which grows in bogmoss under heather. Rock outcrops also have a characteristic flora with yellow-flowered Goldenrod, the neat comb-like fronds of Polypody Fern and the white, grey, yellow or brown of encrusting lichens that completely cover all exposed areas.

Walkers along tracks on warm summer days become familiar with the sudden flash of iridescent green as Tiger Beetles fly up from the bare earth. Other conspicuous beetles include blundering blue-black Dung Beetles which buzz across the heather and scurrying inch long Violet Ground Beetles and their close relatives. Rarer, but unmistakable with a fat body and soft wing-cases, is the sluggish Oil Beetle.

Large hairy dark brown caterpillars of the Fox Moth are frequently seen on heather; an even larger spiky, brilliant green caterpillar is that of the resplendent Emperor Moth. Most moths only fly at night but moorland does have its compliment of butterflies, including the chequer-patterned Dark Green and Small Pearl-bordered Fritillaries and a speciality of north-west Scotland, the orange and grey Large Heath.

Ground-living insects are an important part of the diet of Common Lizards, most often glimpsed as they dive for cover on a sun-warmed heathery bank. Slow-worms may also be found, usually on short turf at the edge of scrub or woodland. Adders, the only snake found this far north in Britain, are most often seen in spring, when, recently emerged from their winter hibernation, they bask in the sun on grassy banks.

Limestone

The limestone areas, at Inchnadamph, Elphin and Knockan, have been a Mecca for botanists for over 100 years. A good indicator that you are on limestone proper is Mountain Avens which has large and beautiful white flowers, but limestone turf, which is kept short by rabbits sheep and deer, harbours many other small gems, including Viviparous Bistort and Lady's-mantles. In shaded crevices in the rocks are the glossy fronds of Holly Fern and tufts of the delicate Green Spleenwort. Much more difficult to find, since the flowering stems are so often grazed off, are the dusky flowers of the Dark Red Helleborine.

Along the watercourses tiny specialities such as Scottish Asphodel and Variegated Horsetail may be found. Rather easier to see are dark green bushes of Whortle-leaved Willow hanging from vertical rock faces.

Mountains

For the first time visitor the hills often provide the greatest thrill, though their summits are rather sparsely vegetated. The dominant plant is often Woolly Hair-moss, with occasional cushions of Thrift, Moss Campion, Mossy Cyphel and the hardier grasses and sedges. On the slopes leading to the tops occur Mountain Azalea, Alpine Bearberry and the prostrate form of Juniper. In more sheltered spots the creeping stems, shiny leaves and catkins of Britain's smallest shrub, the Least Willow may be found. However, sheltered north-facing cliffs, where base rich gneiss pushes up into the Torridonian and water drips down the cliffs, it is a different story. On the buttresses of Quinag there are hanging gardens of Purple and Yellow Saxifrages with Globeflower and Alpine Saw-wort.

Assynt specialities: Black-throated and red-throated divers

'TYSTIES', 'BONXIES' AND BIRDS OF A FEATHER *Doug Mainland*

Things start to 'hot up' during March, April and early May. Our winter migrants are departing for their breeding grounds; Goldeneye duck to Scandinavia, Pink-footed, Greylag and Barnacle Geese to Iceland and Greenland. Whooper Swans and Great Northern Divers are also heading north while the summer migrants such as Wheatear, Willow Warbler, Common Sandpiper, Swallow and Cuckoo start to arrive and the Red-throated Divers return to nest on small inland lochs.

To enjoy Assynt's special blend of birdlife look out for different species in varios distinct habitats.

Birds of the Coast

The coastal strip which runs from Loch Kirkaig in the south to Loch a Chairn Bhain has its fair share of bays, sea lochs, sandy beaches, rocky shores and cliffs, all holding birds of interest. Cormorants and Shags are regularly seen fishing close to the shore. These 'reptilian' birds are similar in appearance but the larger cormorant has a heavy bill and a patch of yellow skin on its white throat . The slender shag, often seen hanging out its wings to dry, has a smaller patch of white facial skin and makes an obvious jump as it dives for food.

Black-headed, Common, Herring, Lesser Black-backed and Great Black-backed Gulls can all be spotted, both on land and offshore. Look out for the Arctic and Common Terns, surely the most graceful of our seabirds, aptly called sea swallows.

Bonxies - real pirates

A notable feature is the headland that reaches out to the Point of Stoer, a must for any visitor who wishes to see a wide range of seabirds. Here, colonies of Fulmar show their graceful mastery of stiff-

Fulmars nest on cliff ledges

winged flight and Gannets soar up and down the coast. There can be few more spectacular sights than a gannet with white body, black-tipped wings and yellow head, plunging, dart-like, after a fish. There are also nesting Razorbills, Guillemots and the gull-like Kittiwake. Less common but very attractive is the Black Guillemot or 'Tystie' flying in and out from its rocky refuge, distinguished by its black body, white wing patches and bright red legs.

Two sea marauders, the Great Skua and Arctic Skua, can both be seen around Stoer Head. The larger great skua or 'Bonxie' is a stocky brown bird with obvious white flashes on the wing. The more slender Arctic skua has brown wings and underbody colour that varies from very pale to dark brown. Both skuas harry terns and gulls in flight forcing them to drop any food they are carrying which the chasing birds retrieve.

Exclusive to the foreshore, the Rock Pipit is often overlooked as its dark olive brown plumage makes good camouflage against the rocky background.

Our best known sea duck, the Eider, is seen during the breeding season, sometimes in groups or 'rafts' offshore. Like all ducks the female is a fairly dull brown colour. The male eider, though, is very distinctive in black and white with a light green patch on the back of the head.

Sandy beaches are favourite haunts for waders such as the Curlew and Oystercatcher. Have a closer look for the neat Ringed Plover standing motionless, well camouflaged, until it makes its short darting runs in and around the stranded seaweed. Redshank, Dunlin and Turnstone can also be seen from time to time.

Birds of lochs, rivers and burns
Red-breasted Mergansers move, from wintering on the coast, inland to the lochs and river systems. The merganser is the smaller of the two breeding saw-billed ducks in these parts. It is slender in appearance with a long thin bill and double crest. Its larger and bulkier cousin, the Goosander, finds its way on to rivers and large feeder burns to breed. The most widespread duck is the well-known Mallard though there are smaller numbers of Wigeon and Teal with just one or two pairs of Tufted Duck.

The Heron, a large bird that nests colonially both on coastal cliffs and inland in trees, is often seen stalking at the edge of still waters. The Dipper, however, seeks fast flowing burns and rivers. This small, plump, dark bird has a white breast patch and is noted for its bobbing motion while standing on a rock. A very graceful small bird found near fast flowing water is the Grey Wagtail but Reed Buntings prefer the water margins.

North-west Scotland is a stronghold for one of our most spectacular waders, the Greenshank. As well as the light green legs, it can be recognised by a slightly upturned bill and, in flight, a distinctive white wedge up its back. They first appear on the coast in April before moving inland to breed.

The Black-throated Diver is much loved. The wailing cry made as it asserts its territory can be one of the most haunting sounds ever heard. This goose-sized bird has an obvious black throat bordered by stripes and is most likely to be seen at a distance cruising gracefully on the larger lochs or diving for fish.

The black-throated diver population is closely monitored by the Royal Society for the Protection of Birds in an attempt to increase the breeding success of this all too easily disturbed, summer visitor to freshwater lochs.

Birds of moor and mountain

The grey and black Hooded Crow is widespread in the area. South of the Great Glen it is seen as the all black Carrion Crow. The largest member of the crow family is the glossy black Raven which breeds in good numbers in the area. Unmistakable because of its large size, wedge shaped tail and heavy bill ravens, are often seen flying in pairs over sheep walks with a beautiful undulating flight.

Open moorlands hold Wheatear, Twite, Whinchat, Stonechat and the most common small bird, the Meadow Pipit. The meadow pipit is important because it is the main food source for some of our birds of prey.

Birds of prey

Raptors always generate excitement - everyone wants to see a Golden Eagle. For a big bird it is extremely elusive, shunning all human disturbance. So, anyone hoping to see one will have to walk out into the remoter glens and hills. The age old question of whether it is a buzzard or an eagle still comes up. If in doubt, it's a buzzard, sorry but eagles are not seen on the tops of telephone poles.

Buzzards are our most common bird of prey, soaring over all parts of Assynt apart from very high ground. The Kestrel and Sparrowhawk are also found locally in suitable habitats while the robust Peregrine Falcon can be seen both on the coast and inland. The smallest of our breeding falcons, the dashing little Merlin may only be spotted by a lucky few - a glimpse of the blackbird sized male with slate blue back or the brown female with her cream barred tail. Our rarest breeding raptor is the Hen Harrier which breeds inland and may be seen quartering ground for prey near roads. Two nocturnal birds to listen out for are the Tawny and Long-eared Owls. The only owl that hunts by day is the Short-eared Owl, flying low over the moors on moth-like wings.

Above: Greenshank
Below: Merlin family

Good luck with your bird watching.

The following birds are listed under schedule I of the Wildlife and Countryside Act 1981 and are afforded special protection at all times.

Black-throated diver, Red-throated diver, Golden eagle Greenshank, Hen harrier, Merlin Peregrine falcon, Redwing

Where eagles fly

TALES - SHORT AND TALL *Kenny Mackenzie*

The Black Dog of Loch an Ordan

In days gone by, travel between the Stoer peninsula and Lochinver was by foot or by cart and perhaps bicycle. It was not unknown for some travellers to take time off at the end of their visit to Lochinver to call at the local hostelry to fortify themselves for the journey home, and it was usually on these return journeys that they came across the Black Dog of Loch an Ordan. He was reputed to be a fearsome sight - enough to sober up the most enthusiastic imbiber! Unfortunately, the advent of the motor car seems to have frightened off the dog, but visitors of a strong disposition might care to re-enact the old formula in the hope of reviving the legendary beast!

According to a local bard, this is what they would see:
With eyes ever searching the side of the hill.
He went striding along, then with horror stood still.
From a rock at his side
A black shadow did glide.
Twas as big as a cow.
And he saw plainly now
That confronting him there,
With eyes all aglare
Was the terrifying Dog of Craig n'ordan.
The Dog was indeed a fell monster of dread.
With eyes shining forth like the light on Stoer Head.

From his gaping jaw hung
A red flame of a tongue,
While his great teeth shone bright
In its awful red light.
And his sulphurous breath
Seemed to herald the death
To be dealt by the Dog of Craig n'ordan

An old woman of Stoer (Mary Macleod) relates how a relative of hers met the dog. He was proceeding along the road when he heard splashing in the loch and saw in the moonlight a big black dog with burning eyes coming out of the loch towards him. The animal growled and spat sparks at him. He fled in terror and the dog followed. When it at last overtook him and looked back he saw a hideous human face surmounted by horns. The dog trotted in front for a while till suddenly it gave a peal of 'diabolical' laughter and vanished through the centre of the road.

Coffin Stones

Alongside the roads at various points in Assynt are stones reputed to have a strange effect on passing animals, especially horses. Two of the best known are at Alt-na-brahan and Elphin. Not too many horses pass these places nowadays, but in days of old, there were many reported incidents of horses refusing to move a step past these rocks and having to be unyoked and their heads covered before they could be coaxed past.

Is it coincidence that these same rocks were also recognised as resting places for coffins when coffins were carried by hand, many miles, in procession, to the distant burial grounds?

Altnacealgach (the burn of the cheat).

Assynt forms the southern boundary between Sutherland and Ross-shire, and in days gone by, when the exact line dividing the two counties was disputed, two old Ross-shire men walked the marches: "Mind", they were warned, "your feet are on oath". At the end of their walk, they claimed they had never once left Ross-shire soil. Nor had they, for they had taken the precaution of filling their shoes with earth from Balnagowan in Easter Ross before setting off.

Their guile is remembered to this day in the name of the burn at the county boundary on the road from Bonar Bridge.

The Curse of Kylesku

After a shipwreck many years ago a keg of whisky was washed ashore at Kerrachar Bay in Loch Cairnbawn. It was found and taken to the old Ferryhouse (now the hotel) at Kylesku by a fisherman nicknamed Tordeas. He left it in an upstairs room, entered by a wooden loft ladder, on the west side of the Inn.

While he and several friends drank the contents of the cask a 'seer' present foretold a great calamity but was not believed. A drunken argument developed and Tordeas protested that Sunday was approaching.

His son, losing his temper, pushed Tordeas, who fell headlong down the stairs. The fall broke his neck and he died screaming, 'My son, I shall return to have my revenge'. The son was found drowned in Loch Glencoul a few weeks later.

Each year at midnight, on the anniversary of the happening, Tordeas is said to appear at the entrance of the hotel 'snuggery' below the loft ladder.

The Brown Lady

The Brown Lady is said to appear on a bend of the road beside Loch Drumbeg just on the west side of Drumbeg village. She appears as a woman dressed completely in brown and walks across the road before disappearing.

Assynt Light

This is seen off the coast out at sea. It is locally called 'Teine'. It has been observed to travel at speed and is believed to foretell disaster. From the Assynt shore it is known as 'Solus MhicAloidh'. Seen from Kinlochbervie it is called the 'Assynt Light' (Teine Assynt). The cause remains a mystery.

The Maiden's Tresses

The local name for Eas Coul Aulin originates in the tale of an Assynt girl betrothed to a man she did not love. To avoid an unhappy marriage she hid along the cliffs of Leitir Dhubh. When a party was sent out to bring her back she threw herself over the edge and her tresses spread out to form the waterfall.

THROUGH YOUNG EYES

Assynt

Assynt is a great place to be
Lots of things to view and see
Rugged mountains
And waterfall fountains
And you can go to the splashing sea.
You can see the Kylesku bridge
And get bitten by the Midge
You can see in the sky
The eagles fly
And get some fresh salmon for your fridge.

Holly Lockie
Drumbeg Primary School
Aged 9

PLACES TO VISIT .... IN ASSYNT

Please remember when taking a closer look at some of the features and heritage of Assynt to treat them with respect, and so help conserve them for future generations.

Knockan Visitor Centre

Nature trail, geological trail and, during the summer, a visitor centre where information on the neighbouring Inverpolly National Nature Reserve is available.

Inchnadamph Reserve

Covering the 3000-acre plateau between Stronchrubie cliffs and Breabag, the area is well-known for its rich and varied plant life and the multitude of cave systems.

Alt a Chalda Beag Crushing Mill

Opposite Ardvreck Castle, near the lay-by. The large mill wheel was used in a vertical position, probably ox driven. A small quarry nearby provided the limestone that when crushed was used for road works and as a fertiliser to improve poor land.

Ardvreck Castle

Built in 1597 by the MacLeods. In 1691 the Seaforth Mackenzies laid siege to the castle to enforce the payment of a debt and ejected the Macleods. By 1736 the Mackenzie

Laird was forced to sell the land to pay his debts and it finally was bought by Lady Strathnaver in 1757 and given to her grandson the Earl of Sutherland.

Calda House

Built in 1695 by the first Mackenzie laird of Assynt. In 1737 Calda House mysteriously burnt down and, although the Earl of Seaforth, who was in violent dispute with the Earl of Sutherland over ownership, was accused, nothing was ever proved.

Lochinver Harbour

The returning fishing fleet can be seen unloading their catch in the evening. A pleasant walk is to be found near-by, along the White Shore path through the Culag wood-land.

Falls of Kirkaig

From the bridge over the River Kirkaig a path leads east to the Falls of Kirkaig (about 2 miles) and on to the south side of Suilven.

Alltan na Bradhan

Coastal walk from the beach car park at Achmelvich to an old meal mill with mill wheels and mill-race still visible. The mill stones were cut and dressed on Suilven then rolled down the Kirkaig valley. From there, they were taken by boat along the coast. All this was the work of one man, John MacLeod of Stoer. The walk continues northwards to see the Split Rock.

Point of Stoer

The most westerly part of Sutherland provides views of the mountains of Assynt, the rugged Wester Ross coastline and, on a clear day, the Hebrides. A clifftop walk northwards for about 2 miles from the lighthouse car park leads to the impressive 200 foot seastack, the Old Man of Stoer.

Rhu Stoer Lighthouse

Built in 1870 by two brothers, David and Thomas, of the famous Stevenson family. It is no longer manned, having been automated in 1976.

Eas Coul Aulin

200 metres high, this is the highest waterfall in Britain. The name means 'the splendid waterfall of Coul'. Boat trips to see the falls and local wildlife leave from Kylesku or experienced walkers can approach from Loch na Gainmhich.

... AROUND AND ABOUT ASSYNT

Oldshoremore and Oldshorebeg
Rich dune grasslands or 'machairs' and beautiful sandy beaches.

Faraid Head and Balnakiel
An extensive sand dune system, excellent bird-watching, 9-hole golf course, ruined church and craft village cluster together in this north-west corner.

Cape Wrath
The Clo Mor, which in Gaelic means 'Great Web' or 'Great Cloth', is the highest cliff in mainland Britain and has huge colonies of seabirds. Access is via passenger ferry from Keoldale and a mini-bus service.

Smoo Cave, Durness
Probably the largest cave entrance in Britain. Inside, the Allt Smoo tumbles over 60 feet through one of the openings in the roof.

Sandwood Bay
A 4 mile walk to one of the loveliest and loneliest beaches in Scotland. Legends tell of mermaids and the ghost of the 'Bearded Sailor'.

Handa
This nature reserve, wardened by the Scottish Wildlife Trust, provides a home for over 100,000 breeding seabirds. From Tarbet a regular ferry service operates daily, though not on Sundays or in rough weather.

Achiltibuie and the Summer Isles
Sea cruises, Smokehouse produce and Hydroponicum in an enchanting corner of Wester Ross

Inverpolly Nature Reserve
The second largest National Nature Reserve in Great Britain includes the sandstone peaks of Cul Mor, Cul Beag and Stac Pollaidh.

Falls of Kirkaig

Summer seas

FURTHER READING:

The Sutherland Book. Ed. Donald Omand. Pub. The Northern Times Ltd., Golspie.

Assynt Geological Motor Trail. D.R. Shelley. Pub. Sutherland Tourist Board.

Prehistoric Lochbroom and Assynt. Cathy Dagg.

Flowering plants and ferns of Lochbroom and Assynt. Colin Scouller.

John Anthony's Flora of Sutherland. J.B. Kenworthy.

Sutherland Birds. Ed. Stewart Angus. Pub. The Northern Times Ltd., Golspie.

Making more of Assynt. Bill Ritchie. Assynt Mountain Rescue Team.

The Northwest Highlands. D.J. Bennet & T. Strang. The Scottish Mountaineering Trust.

Collected Poems. Norman MacCaig. Chatto and Windus.

Macgregor and Phemister's Geological Excursion Guide to the Assynt district of Sutherland. M.R.W. Johnson & I. Parsons. Edinburgh Geological Society.

Highland Geology Trail. John L. Roberts. Pub. Strathtongue Press.

Portrait of Caithness and Sutherland. James Miller. Pub. Robert Hale.

John Home's Survey of Assynt. Ed. R.J. Adam Edinburgh.

Survey of Parishes of Assynt and Eddrachillis. Adam & Rankin. Inverness.

COUNTRYSIDE AND MOUNTAIN CODES

1. Guard against all risk of fire
2. Leave all gates as you find them, open or closed
3. Keep dogs under proper control
4. Keep to the footpaths
5. Be careful not to damage hedges, fences or walls
6. Leave no litter
7. Safeguard water supplies
8. Do not disturb wildlife or stock

Between mid-August and mid-October there are stalking parties on the hills. Enquire locally to ensure access is safe.

Anyone attempting to climb the mountains should carry (and be able to use) a map and compass, torch, spare food and first aid kit. Always carry warm clothes and waterproofs and wear the proper footwear.

Leave a note of your proposed route and estimated time of return with the local police, your landlady, hostel warden, neighbour or friend and **don't forget to tell them when you do get back.** A standard form is available from the Tourist Information Centre.

The Tourist Information Centre, Lochinver can provide any further information or advice.

ACKNOWLEDGEMENTS:

The Assynt Tourism Group would like to take this opportunity of thanking Caithness and Sutherland Enterprise and the Sutherland Tourist Board for their financial assistance in producing this book.

Photography:
A. Burrows, I. Evans, P. Evans, N. Kerr, S. Nairn, C. MacFarlane, S. MacLeod, C. Pellant, T. Strang, G. Rebecca, W. Ritchie, RSPB, Sutherland Tourist Board

Archive photographs:
A. McCall, M. Klein

Artwork:
Maps by G. Allighan. Original line drawings by P. Phillips

The publishers would particularly like to thank the contributors and guest authors for their generous and valuable assistance during the preparation of this book, and to Nick Kerr for his exhaustive efforts, pulling the whole thing together.

Typing:
R. Dutton, F. MacAulay.

Translation:
R. Lindsay, C. Tutzschky, A.R. Matran, A. Clausse, A. MacPhail.

Origination by Hiscan, Inverness